About the Author

Misty Barber is an author residing in Australia who, through her love for words and stories, developed a passion for writing. *Secrets We Don't Keep* is the sequel to Barber's first book, *Things We Say in the Night*.

Secrets We Don't Keep

Misty Barber

Secrets We Don't Keep

Olympia Publishers
London

www.olympiapublishers.com
OLYMPIA PAPERBACK EDITION

Copyright © Misty Barber 2024

The right of Misty Barber to be identified as author of
this work has been asserted in accordance with sections 77 and 78 of
the Copyright, Designs and Patents Act 1988.

All Rights Reserved

No reproduction, copy or transmission of this publication
may be made without written permission.
No paragraph of this publication may be reproduced,
copied or transmitted save with the written permission of the publisher,
or in accordance with the provisions
of the Copyright Act 1956 (as amended).

Any person who commits any unauthorised act in relation to
this publication may be liable to criminal
prosecution and civil claims for damage.

A CIP catalogue record for this title is
available from the British Library.

ISBN: 978-1-80439-965-1

This is a work of fiction.
Names, characters, places and incidents originate from the writer's
imagination. Any resemblance to actual persons, living or dead, is
purely coincidental.

First Published in 2024

Olympia Publishers
Tallis House
2 Tallis Street
London
EC4Y 0AB

Printed in Great Britain

The Ruining

Pretty,
The word we are so desperate to be
The word we cry and cry over to feel
The word that makes us barrel over each other
And reach out with crushing weights pounding each of us behind.

Just to be pretty,
We drown ourselves in colours
And fragrance.

To be of beauty
Means we can't breathe
Our bones are broken,
Organs crushed together
To hold childlike inches.

But it's never enough
We're never good enough for the word,
But we spend our whole lives dying to feel considered it.

To those who only live to read another page
Whose lives are done in routine
But never with feeling.

They only exist to feel through other people
To be titled as a viewer for as long as they should remain.

Maybe this is what life is all about,
All of this disappointment
And heartache
Over and over again,
Maybe I'll find a way to be okay with it all
To be able to put some meaning behind it,
So that all these feelings and aggressions
Weren't for nothing.

But for now
I harbour those feelings
And have made a home for them
Somewhere deep in my body,
Maybe there will be no significance to this pain
In any future day
And I'll sit through my old ages,
Wondering why I cared so much.

I'm sick of the past chasing me around
In circles that I can't pace,
Begging me to keep up with it
So, I don't look out for anything else.

It's a race I'll never win
So, I continue in pursuit
That whatever has me running,
Will come and take my place.

I'm exhausted of trying to be perfect
Putting ointment on cracked skin
And guarding my stomach till it becomes paper thin,
It's all an attempt to fix everything
Hoping someone notices
And thinks it's beautiful.

But each day I scrub
And sweat till my heart starts to throb in my head
Nobody sees it,
Only I do
Which isn't enough anymore.

There's not a thing I wouldn't do
To avoid being invisible.

I'm trying not to hide behind anything
But it feels like I'm just trying
To be all these little somethings,
Just waiting for things to happen.

But the more I wait
The more days that go by like nothing
And I've unfilled a million
Empty promises.

I often think about things I would tell you,
Details about my life
That only you would understand,
But you were awful to me
And somehow,
I miss you even though
All that hurt is the only thing that is now left.

The boy that I spoke to again
That I couldn't shut up about,
The fight I had
With a person you couldn't stand,
Such mundane things that I can't tell
anyone else,
So, I have to whisper them to myself.

Some days we had together were so simple,
Driving till we ran out of petrol
And watching a TV show that just came out,
Then there were the other days
Where you would yell at me
Till I looked away and blinked so hard,
To stop myself from breaking down.

I wish there was an in-between,

Some way to help me put together
How you could be so protective and cruel,
All at the same time
But one day I'll make peace with it all,
In some way that leaves you completely out.

You used me
Not for the first time
And certainly not the last,
But I'd do anything you asked
To finally be under your attention.

Feet are dragging my body weight
Except I can't feel a thing
Corners of lips are dragged down,
Goosebumps are spread throughout for no particular reason.

It's hard to do anything when I've taken a backseat
And let everything else take control,
I feel abandoned
And sick of telling people things about myself.

I've given it all up
Just to spite myself,
Now everyone looks at me funny
Like I'm always striking a nerve.

I hate the way it sits in my stomach
Reminding myself that I'll always look like this,
Poking at my skin till it's forced to stick out
My mind cursing me for not holding a stronger battle.

Except defeat is one I'm used to
And I've given up all my self-control
The second it's gone down,
Till I'm hunched over
Begging for it to make its way out.

Sometimes I contemplate if people forget that women can be wholesome,
Or be innocent and exist for no one else,
For as long as I can remember
It seemed that when you turned fourteen,
sexuality was washed over you
And nothing was pure anymore.

People then only knew you for dirtiness
And how well puberty had passed you by,
We were conditioned to only be loved
By those that didn't care
Or just saw us as a body count.

It made me sad that as a girl
I had to get over the idea of someone touching my hands
And stopping at that,
Or for once asking before they took and ruined something.

You said some awful words
In order to describe me
Your friends laughed and you egged them on
Telling them every detail,
Information that crossed between both lies and the truth.

I heard every venomous word
And looked down at the ground
My reflection staring up at me,
Wishing I truly knew you before I trusted you.

I tried so hard to the very core of my existence
To make sure you never got mad at me,
Always making sure that no was never a part of my
Vocabulary
And I defended your honour to anyone,
Those that had ears.

You raised your voice too many octaves high
Something made you mad
So, you aimlessly throw that at me.

I look at you confused
Asking why you are hurling stones in my direction,
But you don't feel bad
You never do
So, you just shout some more
Till I crouch down as small as I can.

Every year, I change my clothes
Adapt to be something else
Colour my hair
And become a different version of myself,
I'm always running away from who I've been
Changing the songs, I listen to
And the movies I say are my favourite.

It's a bit of an act we all do
Curating the perfect description of ourselves
Telling people, we like these things
So, they think we are cool,
Creating an essay like speech about things we hate
And sharing opinions we pick-pocketed,
From other people.

After each day of pretending to the outside world
Plastering fake smiles,
I collapse onto the same bed I've always slept on
Although it has different sheets
And I think about how much I'm not prepared for tomorrow.

Then when I wake,
I carry myself to the daylight
Existing as if I never thought what I had the day before,
But ready to tuck myself into the same midnight thoughts.

I'll spend half of my time
Building up the courage
To be worth your while,
Imagining that I might be something
You could want around.

Things can change you
Colours can paint you
You can grow big and small
And you can change your hair when you get bored,
But you'll always remember what happened.

You can't get rid of it,
The memories
And all the time it took to accept it
Even if you become addicted to injections,
To get so far away from the girl that it happened to.

Even the time that doesn't stop the lines from forming,
But traps you in those memories,
Till the day comes where you don't recognise
Who you're looking at in the mirror
But you know what happened to her.

My lips are the most abandoned part of me
They don't feel a thing
And are mostly unseen,
I imagine what it would feel like for them to be touched from someone
Instead of the ghost-thin air that is always too cold.

If I damaged the skin
It would make no difference,
Because they could explore every shade and texture
Without a single witness.

There's something deep inside me
Being torn apart,
It's been happening for a while
And it's chaotic and loud,
It creates more space for things to fall out.

I've been with this hole for some years now
But the deeper it digs,
The more I become afraid that it will never be filled again
So, I take the shovel before it can commit a crime itself
And I hide inside,
Terrified that whatever I choose next might bury me alive.

Forgive me for hiding,
But I can't repair anything it's been too long since before it
To which I no longer remember what was before,
Or maybe it's always been there
and I was just too naïve to decipher
Those silent parts of me.

You have a way of making me feel so dirty
I'll cover up but you'll still call me things
I'll wash my body numb,
To clean off your damage
But you've managed to stain me.

You make me feel so cruel
With your tears
And your pleas,
Even though you would push me into harm
If it benefitted yourself.

I am a disease
a horribly contagious one
so, people don't come near
because they're scared,
they'll become
anything like me.

You were the exception
A fearless pretender,
Your steps were so close and inviting
And for some time
You invaded my life,
Begging me to make you as disgusting as I am
So, I let you consume me.

Soon you recovered
Washed yourself clean
And threw me out,
Reminding me that even though someone tried
It would never work out in the long run.

My stomach aches sometimes
Consumed by wondering why I'm so lonely
And why everyone seems to be so happy
Or living such a normal life.

I'm so tired of living on the outside
Of friendships,
Secret parties,
Stolen kisses and broken out belly laughs.

How did I get kicked out of something I never got to experience?
Is reading stories of others going to suffice,
Because it's all I have
Living vicariously through people,
Who are stuck inside a paper book.

I hate reflections
Where stolen glances are taken briefly
And I see myself staring back.

It's at those times when I wish I never left my hiding spot,
Just to let people see the ugliness I take up
Or even worse
How achingly average I am.

It'd be better to be placed on one side
of the spectrum of adjectives,
Then a forgotten pile of those you don't notice in a crowd.

I can't even bring myself to look in the mirror
Because I'm afraid I'll break the glass,
How easy it was to forget what she looked like the last time
And convince myself that in the passing of time,
I was transformed
When I hadn't changed,
Not one bit at all.

There's so much of me that wanted to stand out
Or at least feel comfortable in all that I am,
But something always feels wrong
And I'm so tired of changing something,
Every two months
Or having a crisis that fills me up.

I'll always miss who I was yesterday
Without the thoughts that possessed me today.

I tried,
Again
To weave myself through long-time friends,
Accept invitations,
Try to be myself,
Except it didn't work
Because it never really does
Maybe I forgot to laugh at a joke
Or crossed a line that others know is forbidden.

Why do I keep pushing myself
To be with other people,
When clearly nobody wants me around?

Am I just punishing myself?
Or do I think that somehow,
I'm more extroverted than last time
So maybe people might accept me more.

I'm sick of trying over and over again
Just to be met with the same results
And why am I always left trying to heal myself,
Just to stab the same wounds again.

What if I'll never be okay again,
Will I have to surrender to tear stained cheeks
And dark purple hues,
That hang below
Two distant looking eyes.

Will I always have to feel like this
Trapped in cages I've locked myself in
And how do I set myself free,
When I can't even remember the code
To my own sanity.

I'm not sure how to accept the way I look
But at the same time,
I'm conflicted
Because on the one hand,
I think it's stupid to worry about such artificial matters
But on the other
It's the one thing people notice first,
Above everything else.

Before they understand the different things
That make you laugh,
They notice the amount of space separating
Your eyes
And how many of your teeth have spaces in-between.

While I know I'm no exception to this rule,
I wish I had won my own genetic lottery
Because while there are those that stand out,
With their kind inviting eyes
And perfectly carved bones.

Mine have forgotten the memo
So instead of kind,
My eyes contain a sense of dullness and jealousy
And my bones have woven themselves
Somewhere across,
crooked and incomplete.

I've never been able to let go of things
Or forgive people when it's due,
I don't know why I can't
But I know that the resistance takes up
Every bit inside of me.

I wish I could accept
When things happen
And move on within an appropriate timeline,
But I can't
Because I always end up stuck in the middle,
Too wound up in remembering
The smallest of things.

I'm so tired of saying anything
Of overused words,
Rehearsed and repeated
Said like it holds any meaning.

Why do I have to talk anyway
When none of it implies much,
There isn't a reply I could make
That could fix the problem
Or make you laugh
So, why do I bother with boring conversations.

Sometimes I stare too hard at the words
Coming out of someone's mouth,
Listening to the obscurity
That is the English language,
Made up by a random curator
That travelled to our tongues,
only to be used
For entirely the wrong reasons.

I don't make much indifference
And when I speak most don't hear it,
I'll stand back and watch others have their moment
Too afraid of endless outcomes.

I tune out the volume
That comes from being around you,
I'm almost always alone
Tiring myself with made up conversations.

I go to bed without anyone asking
And I roll around till the sun comes up,
Just to do it all again
Hoping one of these days will eventually end.

I'm hiding because if I do
Then I have a reason to be ignored,
It makes sense for no one to speak to me
Or ignore me
Because I am by myself.

As soon as I step outside
The only excuse I have behind
Fading into the background,
Is because there are too many faults
In my personality.

I wish I could tape my mouth shut
And never mutter a single word ever again,
I hate my own sound
And I cringe at the noise it makes.

All I ever do is say the most uninteresting of things
Or try to be funny
So shut me up,
Before I offend you
Or even worse I bore you.

Sometimes on bad days,
I think about your childhood home
And how there's a piece of me,
Constantly haunting every corner of it
Still to this day.

Growing up didn't see us through
And if we were to see each other again today,
We would be strangers again
But on occasions, I'll imagine us having a conversation,
As the kids we once were
And it's probably the best conversation I've had
In years.

I have a memory of us,
That is always stuck on repeat in my head
The day everyone thought the world was ending,
It broadcasted all over the news
So I put on my colourful shoes
And walked to your house,
We laughed so loud that all the talk on the TV,
Became nothing but static.

I've been on both sides of things
Through everything,
I've walked this path when I was content
And the same path when I felt overbearingly lonely.

But on every side
I never once met myself,
in the middle.

I'm looking in the mirror
And all I can see are the extra linings
To each of my parts
Instead of anything that truly counts,
I feel as if every part of my body is wrong
Like there is a way a muscle should be shaped
And then there is mine.

It's in me like a second skin
To be this uncomfortable,
Having these insecurities guarding me
From doing anything,
Telling me that rejection is my only answer.

I get motivated
And then I break down
I start again
Just to collapse once it ends.

How do I break out of this cycle of
self-obliteration,
Am I ever going to accept that I
Will always look like this
And why do I care,
About something so superficial?

I'm nothing too special
And I don't know why I have such a burning desire
To feel it,
There isn't a talent I have
That could amaze everyone,
A personality trait I carry
That draws people into wanting more,
Or a feature on my face
That nobody can resist staring at.

What am I supposed to do with that?
Am I just going to be an admirer
For the rest of my life,
But never be noticed
Or have my turn.

I want to be loud,
To make them all face me
And come near me,
But I'm afraid I'll embarrass myself
So, I shove my hands in front of my mouth
To resist the temptation.

I miss my naivety,
When I could still think of made-up situations
And have some hope,
That one day they would happen.

I'll never get that back
The excitement I had,
To grow up.

I'll never be fifteen again,
Running down midnight streets
While our parents were still asleep.

There will just always be an after
Where I'm stuck in this mind and body I can't stand,
Hiding behind styles and aesthetics
When I just want to be a child.

When I used to be able to count my birthday candles
On only two hands,
All I wanted was to add more
To be like the cool girls I watched on TV.

Except now that I've grown similar in age,
It's anything but cool
And all I want to do is minus the flames,
Travel back to that little girl
Just to trap her in time.

There is nothing worse than saying goodbye to your childhood,
Waking up every day
Till time lapses into,
insignificant years
And you don't remember where it all went,
But you know you would kill to do it all again.

The mirror becomes a stranger
And each year turns into less of a celebration,
Then you're passed out
On every occasion
Because you can't bear to do it sober.

People's desires have made everyone mad,
We base our entire worth
On how many people touch our skin
Or stare at our lips,
But we never care when someone important
Says we are fine just the way we are.

There's a requirement for everything,
A thigh size that you must have
And a reduced stomach,
That saves no room for food to settle in.

And at the end of the night
After every procedure and meaningless kiss,
You go home to a different face in the mirror
Trapping who you really are,
In almost forgotten memories.

Everything I do,
Is done
Just to fill the time,
I'll make plans I could care less about
And I go to sleep.

Not because I'm tired
But because I want to be knocked out,
For a little while.

I fall in love with strangers
I'll never meet again,
Toxins slide down my throat
And things become blurry,
Then these strangers kiss me
Even though I don't know what to call them.

I bask in their touches
Because I know I won't receive them in the morning,
We're just playing pretend for the night
As if we are some couple,
It's fun that way
Knowing we'll never see each other again
But it leaves me wondering what it all feels like,
When it actually means something.

Once I'm alone
I can't wait to do it all again
As soon as the moon makes an appearance,
I'm not sure if I enjoy it anymore
Or if I'm just overcompensating for something.

My whole life I've been scared of everything,
Like dancing shadows
And standing up in front of crowds,
Every fear I have
Has me in a chokehold
Terrified to make the next move,
Anticipating a final blow.

I hate being so terrified constantly,
My lungs too deprived of air
Leaving my throat an abandoned passageway,
Why am I so incompetent of becoming my own hero
Will I always rely on something to save me?

Fear owns me
And without wanting to
I've become its biggest fan.

There wasn't a harder challenge for me to do
Then walking past everyone I'd ever been
And never seeing a single version again,
I try to dress up as them
To bring them back to life,
But they tell me to move on
That it's time for me to grow a new skin.

I miss the friends I had
That are now nothing but strangers
I miss living in a fantasy,
Believing in stupid things,
Now I don't have anything I can hold onto
That feels as simple as what once was.

I don't have my fairy godmother
Because she never existed
And the books I received
From passed away relatives,
Are sitting on shelves
Drowning in dust.

I was put into this world
Expected to have perfect measurements
And dips,
But I failed horribly
And all I can do is watch those that managed to do it right.

It's all so effortless for them
They live through their life
Like it's a dance,
Constantly expecting the best to come
And never fearful of rejection,
I look like a fool next to them
endlessly begging for a compliment,
hoping that maybe I'm just not seeing something about myself
that comes from another person's perspective.

So, while they shine like beautiful ornaments,
I step back and watch them perform like everyone else
Wishing I was born like them,
Wishing I could be the centre of someone's attention
Without having to make a fool of myself.

There is a deep unsettled feeling
Attached to my gut,
Telling me that it's never going to happen for me
That I'll never experience what everyone else seems destined for,
The sacred spaces,
Warm heartbeats,
And secret smiles.

I've grown up
And stopped dreaming of scenarios that are too late to happen now,
I've heard the words it will happen eventually
And there is someone for everyone
As if it's a prayer to my lips.

I have written in journals
Worked at myself like a full-time job
While stomping on the ground I walk on,
Frustrated in agony that I continue living this way
With no one to share a life with.

Waiting has a permanent seat
My name scratched on it for eternity,
I'm trying to hold onto what little hope I do have left

Pretending I don't care
And telling people when it finds me it finds me.

But they don't know I look for it in the most mundane of things,
I look for you
Hoping you exist
And that you hurry up and come meet me already,
So, I can love someone like I've always wanted to.

I don't think I'll ever be ready for it
But it's all anyone ever talks about,
I don't think I'll enjoy it, but you can't get a fairy-tale ending
Without it,
I'm afraid I'll lose all of myself
That I'll come out the other side as a stranger
And that I won't be okay after.

I am depleted
And I'll never know how to explore this part of myself,
I just want to feel normal
Fearless of experiences
And not like a coward,
Who's decided against things
Before taking part in them.

I'll always be alone
Even when there is someone there,
No one will ever be in my mind with me
I'll always be covering things up,
Lying and saying the wrong thing
Struggling to read people
and feeling exhausted from their reactions.

There is no one that makes me feel like I'm not obscure
Like I belong on this hill,
I'll always be on the outside
Faking memories of what others must have felt.

I belong where the dust falls,
Where the silent one's crash
And book pages are more appreciated than
A breath of fresh air.

I try so hard
For people, I don't even like
To not think badly of me,
I slave away trying to create this reputation
That they don't even care about,
I just swallow the words they say
Confused at why theirs come out harsh
With too many rough edges.

I pay attention to every look
That gets thrown at me,
The pitch of every voice I hear
How many words are spilled out
And whether they're said with enthusiasm.

I'm utterly exhausted
At this reading into everything,
Trying way too much for people that I think are awful
And I don't know how to stop
Because I'm on some impossible mission,
To make everyone like me.

Growing up is so odd sometimes,
One year you're begging your parents to buy you
New runners
So that you can run, jump and dance
And you're wearing full length T-shirts,
That you don't particularly care about
And you're stuffing your face when you can
Just because you love the way it tastes,
Or the way it makes you jump so high you can feel the sky
In your hands.

Then in one year, you learn about skin
And bumps,
How much skin to show or how little of it you can get away with
Because suddenly people crave you,
Your young bones and youthful face
And it's exciting until suddenly it isn't,
Till you forget to taste
When food becomes a distant memory
And you don't dance anymore,
But you wish you did.

In one year,
You're a tiny adult

Learning about awful things
When you could have stayed one more year
In your funny looking trainers,
With your wild outgrown hair.

Somewhere along changing
You lose yourself in so many ways,
Leaving increments of who you used to be,
Spread out in too many places
And then suddenly you don't value your kindness
Over your appearance.

I used to have bleached blonde hair,
Wear ugly skirts,
Collect crystal bracelets by the dollar
And work at an ice cream stand.

I used to sing songs I wrote
And with every flat sound
That came out of my mouth,
Still had me believing I could perform on stages.

I used to stand in the mirror
And practice my acceptance speech
For best director,
Staring myself down
Annoyed about how many pimples I had.

I used to dance
Till my bones felt like they were made of electricity,
Believing that I was a sight to see
When I was probably hitting all the wrong moves.

I used to run till my heart collapsed
Because I thought it would make me thinner
And I would eat rabbit food,
Ignoring the way my stomach screamed out.

I used to be a lot of things
All at once
Filled to the brim with hope
With every new thing I tried,
I wish I could capture each wish I had
Into the palm of my hand
And teach myself to dream as big,
As my adolescent self
had.

I cry when you go to sleep
And I pine when you can't see.

How are you supposed to know
When a phase of your life ends,
Before you're really out of it?

Am I just expected to move on all the time,
With no consideration for what has been
And create something new
In order to move forward?

I just want to stay solid for a second,
But I'm always saying goodbye to myself
And never welcoming whatever comes next.

My shoes are always gaining holes
And becoming smothered with dirt,
So I'll go buy another pair
And become something else.

I never know if someone new
Is going to end up meaning that much to me,
So, I'm always the one leaving
Before I give it a chance
Because I can't take the anticipation,
Just for my time to be wasted.

I was stuck back in the void
When I thought I had finally gotten myself out,
But it swallowed me whole
And I wanted to give up this time
Because I was so tired of wasting myself
And becoming a person,
that lacked everything.

I thought I had people holding their hands out
To make sure I wouldn't fall back in,
But they turned their backs
And walked away,
Devoting themselves to someone new.

What even am I to you
If not something you can walk all over,
If I stop playing that part
Will we even be anything?

I should walk away for the last time,
Leaving you in the dust
To just be mean to yourself
But I always come back like your little fan girl,
Begging you to be mean to me again.

I felt torn down
Like I had lost every bit of sanity
I thought I had summoned left,
Loving you without you being aware
Had me turn into a person I didn't even know
I could become.

But I surrendered countless times
To your unrequited torture
Without you having the faintest idea.

It was becoming impossible to hide
That every time you walked into a room
I was jumping over every table,
In hopes of having a conversation.

I try to ignore all of it
Every pang in my chest
Every wince that takes over my face,
I don't want to think about how far away I am
To where it all began
anymore.

I want to be able to accept that time has past
And that I can't change the fact
That I'm moving on,
But somewhere along the way
I became someone afraid of being anything.

Time has turned me into a coward
And I'm bitter for so much of it,
For the inevitable forces that always come
And strip you away from every single good thing,
You had going for you.

When we were friends
I always begged that you'd be better,
You were always so awful to me
But I had an everlasting soft spot for you
Because I was somehow hypnotised
By too many memories,
Into thinking that you were a good person.

Except I was always reminded time and time again
That your efforts ran dry,
almost next to non-existent
and our conversations looked more like me talking,
to myself in my own mirror.

Years made you more unkind
And had you swallowed into too many obsessions,
I always wanted you to treat me
Like I had to you
But all my wishes were never once answered.

You were my own bully
But it was always mislabelled as you being honest,
I always had so many words and sharp sounds
That I could have said to you,
But each time I tried
My mouth was taped shut.

There were so many words people threw at me
Every waking minute
Somehow, they always found the words to say
While I was struggling to remember basic nouns.

I thought if I trapped myself in my room for long enough
People would forget how to talk
And I could be free,
That I could exist without it being anyone's problem.

Everyone always made me get carried away
Through fast-paced closeness,
That wasn't really built on any foundations
And each time it happened
I was convinced that that was it,
I had found people I was supposed to have in my life.

The only problem was,
I was always destined to be wrong
To end up alone,
With memories that don't mean much
And I watch them move on,
Just to replace me as if I never really was there
And while I maintain the online check-ups,
None of it means anything of substance.

It's a shame to let all of these hours
Of conversations
And celebrations
All lead up to nothing once more,
But each time it happens I find a piece of me leaving with it.

When you become settled into the silence
You don't look for sound anymore,
Your ears discontinue to search for your name
Being called,
Because it never is.

you practice the words in your vocabulary
or else your mouth will forget how to pronounce
them.

Everyone around is so deeply invested in the noise
Like you once were,
So you just watch till your eyes give up.

You miss when it was loud
So loud you never thought for a second,
That the noise would run out.

When you're in the middle of it all,
You don't realise that one day you'll wake
And look back at the poor-quality photos,
feeling the sadness trying to swallow you whole.

There are so many things
Counting and depending on this night,
So much hope and anticipation
That could waste away any second,
I don't doubt that you'll disappoint me
But still, I crave it with every way I know how,
To want something.

We are always depending
On accidental encounters
So that no one seems desperate,
Even though I'm painted through
And through with it.

We'll follow our familiar dance
And spend another night together,
That will never go mentioned again
Then like always the morning will make you,
Keep your distance
And it will have all been for nothing,
Until the next time you want me.

I cut my hand
And instead of reacting like I should have,
Instead of putting a bandage around it
I let it fester,
Till it was infected and the pain of it
Became indifferent.

I overreacted to it
And instead of going on with my day,
It became a reason to quietly exist
Until it devoured the time,
So I no longer knew my unadulterated
Hand with perfect scales of skin.

I only knew who I was now
With this wound,
Wishing so desperately that it would go
Away on its own,
Without any help
And wishing that it hadn't happened
In the first place.

Words for Us

It's funny how I could do nothing
If it meant doing it with you
How mundane I could let life become
If you were the one waking me up.

Being with you meant things were simple
In a way that felt natural,
The old me never thought about settling down
Or to let things be calm,
But when we met
Suddenly I could breathe
And nothing sounded better than drinking coffee with you,
Or watching TV.

Whenever your eyes landed on me
I always felt so small,
Your gaze was adoring and constantly made my knees forget their structure
And even though I felt so undeserving of your attention,
Once I had it
I couldn't let it be forgotten.

If we are so forbidden
Why does my hand always find yours
And why do my eyes naturally search,
For your familiar gaze
Tell me,
if it's so not allowed
Why does it feel like everything is exploding
And every problem gets solved when you touch me?

I'm holding you close,
But you're falling through the spaces in my arms
Because feelings are not justified enough for you.

I can only hope that one day we'll meet again
In another world where we could have just been,
Just don't forget me when you're chasing everyone else's dreams.

But in the meantime
I'll light a candle outside of wherever I end up,
In hopes one day, you won't care
And pick me over outdated beliefs

You kissed me
And I hadn't yet experienced liking a kiss
But I liked yours,
It made me realise everything I had been missing
And why movies always end with kissing.

Maybe it isn't as plain and simple as I used to think it was,
It could have been that I was just doing it with the wrong people
Because now that my lips have touched yours,
I don't ever want them to stop.

Half of my thoughts
Are consumed by getting you off my mind
And the other half is spent
Hoping that maybe I'm on yours,
For a fraction of when you're on mine.

I learnt to co-exist with my want
Like an extra limb,
Attached to my body like it never wanted to be
Anywhere else again,
Like I was bound to end up slave to you
From the very start.

It was obvious to anyone who saw me
That part of my personality was shaped into,
Chasing after you
And I begged for anything to replace it
Or a slither of information about you,
To put this desperation to bed.

Each day my feelings just wanted
To spread themselves as wide as any space
I was in,
Till there was no longer room for the rest of me
To fill out.

We are so small
And unknown,
I think everyone should know you
But if they did,
they'd want you for themselves.

And I couldn't line up again
Hoping you'd pick me
Because I'm already covering everyone
In hopes that somebody else,
is not what you need.

You're a song I don't know the words to
Something I want to learn,
That my ears crave to hear again.

I don't want to press pause and hope we interact once more,
I only want to know you now
Because the sound of you,
Has now become a new reoccurring thought
That I don't want to forget.

Does every word that I carefully prepare
Make you happy?

Do you anticipate my syllables?
And look for the octaves that change,
I hope you do.

Or at least appreciate everything I tell you
Because the words I share with you,
Are the only words
That came out of my mouth, that actually
Mean something.

It means everything to me
That above it all,
I'll always have you as someone
Who's not going anywhere.

I know I can't control what happens
In the future,
But I'll be damned if I ever lose you
Because you are the only thing worth fighting for,
The only one I'd trade everything
In this world for.

How does it feel
Knowing that you have me completely,
That I'd lose myself
Before I ever considered letting you go.

I hope you tread carefully
And don't break me
Because even if you were to
Break my every organ and artery,
I'd still be on my knees
Hoping you'd kiss it better.

I'll never not be excited to meet you,
Every day I anticipate the way we'll
Eventually, bump into each other,
It could happen any day now
But I miss you even though I've never met you.

I just know whoever you end up being
Will be perfect for me,
You'll teach me to fall in love
And we'll thank everything
That we met
Because it meant something finally went right.

Cutting it down in hopes you'll draw me back
That little pieces I've given to you,
Have you stupidly waiting for more
Until I don't have to play it cool
And I've made you simply want all of me.

I don't complain when it comes to you
I wait till you answer
And I don't rush you for your time,
Even when you forget about me.

I'm stupid every time
Collapsing under my own self-pity,
But all is left behind
When you say you've missed me.

I'll save a quiet place
For us to meet
Somewhere you'd pick,
If you still had a heartbeat.

In case you're still here in another form
I'll make it special,
Play your favourite music
And wear the dress
You always said looked good on me.

You're still around me,
In the way roses grow in gardens
And sunsets occasionally go on for too long,
Although you aren't physically here anymore to see me smile,
You happened in this universe
And when you did,
You were mine.

You once told me
How afraid you were of growing up
And not because you were scared of the future,
But because you didn't want to grow to be
Someone I stopped liking.

You were afraid
But I wasn't,
Not for a second
Because even though we changed what we were wearing,
Every season
And shuffled the jokes we told
Around,
I'll always know the shape of your heart
And the spaces between your fingers,
That belong to me.

I keep you like it's simple
As if we are always in sync
But I'm lying through my teeth,
When I tell others you think like me.

We are pretending we are perfect,
So that we don't have to face being by ourselves
And we put up with the mismatched banter,
With our routined intimacy.

Whatever it was
The unspoken bond we had,
For a brief moment
It was the most exciting thing I had ever,
Experienced.

Mapping out your hands,
Connecting the dots
To all of your beauty spots
And cheeky grins that made us feel childish.

It had us caught up
We knew that we would never work out
So, we made it short
And didn't waste a second apart.

Although it ended
As quick as it came about,
I'm not sure I'll ever feel the same
About another person's hand in mine,
Or the way they laugh.

I accept it all
The bad treatment and the occasional good,
I do it all hoping one day
That the good,
Will overpower the bad
And you won't feel
That you have to get angry at me anymore,
You'll just realise that I make you happy.

I always stay
Thinking one of these days,
You'll appreciate that I was still here
Even when,
Everyone else walked away.

We only speak when we aren't ourselves
And you never want to do anything
That would actually mean something,
You expect me to be okay with these
Business arrangements.

So, I play the part
Pretending I don't care,
When it's all I ever think about.

I'm so tired of the careless act
Of putting all my wants aside,
So you get all that you want
Because I'm being delusional to think,
That if I give you enough
You'll be grateful for it.

You tolerate me
And it's the worst feeling ever,
To know that nothing I say
Brings you fondness,
Although it does cause your eyes to roll
But at least some part of you,
Still reacts to me.

It was an accepted fact
Whenever we went out,
That I trailed behind you
Like an annoying weight,
you couldn't get rid of.

When I was a child,
I always thought that I'd never let someone
Treat me the same
As those that I frowned upon,
But time has made me a hypocrite
And I've settled for the things,
I used to claim to hate.

I can still recall our best days
The ones that outweighed the screaming matches,
Bed sheets with remnants of tear stains
And uncomfortable silences.

Now that we've gone our separate ways,
My mind seems to have only kept those good times intact
And blurred out all of the ways,
We were so very wrong for each other.

When others heard me speak
They didn't care much for it,
I became someone who got labelled off
Straight from the bat.

When you heard me
You looked through every underlining meaning
And begged me to talk more,
It felt so good to be heard properly
Because it had been the first time,
That I had a listener.

I always felt like an idiot,
Whenever I opened my mouth
Because words would tumble out
And people would snicker
Or block their ears.

But you never made me hate talking
You just put your hand to your chin
And said I was the most fascinating person,
You had ever met.

My skin is set aflame
When yours meets it,
I'm terrified of whose move is next
And I'm sucking in my breath.

You're seeing right through me
And I have nothing to hide behind,
But you don't make me feel bad for it.

I'm relying on you
To hold my vulnerability in your hands
And to not shatter it.

Our hearts are beating at all different timings,
You're glowing so much that
It's blinding
And I've never felt more like a human
Until now.

There are very few times we fall for people
In our lives
If we are lucky, it happens more than once
But when it does you can never replicate it
Or force it,
You just have to be in the right place
At the right time.

It helps you sleep,
Leaves you desperate to keep existing,
Makes you smile when you're stuck at work all-day
And reminds you that you still feel,
That you haven't started rotting
And that you still have a pulse
Thumping through from your wrists.

I waited for you
Till I memorised the way my days passed,
You tipped everything upside down
Made me laugh as soon as you opened your mouth,
You drowned me into happiness
Till I forgot what it was like
To only be sad.

There are so many words I could write
That pave the way I'm feeling,
But never enough for me to say
Out loud.

I could write you a letter
Describing all of my thoughts,
Ones that cover the things plaguing my mind
But I could never tell you,
Anything that I really want to say.

You always speak what you're feeling,
But I wish you wouldn't
Because you like crossing the line
And seeing the way I frown.

Sometimes I wish you would write me a letter,
So that I could know if your mind
Keeps any secrets about your feelings,
If you are the same through and through
Or if you're hiding,
Things you wish you could say as well.

You're smoking out the window
And I'm laying down in my own regrets,
You don't like looking at me
And I hate your stench.

Addictions are what you do best
But I'm obsessed with using you as my own
Self-harm,
We never say much
But I still pound on your door
When the sun goes down.

I wanted you to want me
More than I wanted a good night's sleep,
You were keeping me at an arm's distance
And you never did anything that would say you cared much,
About whom I ended up with.

I'll always remain sickly jealous
Of whomever you end up desiring,
I waste inside
Wondering why I wasn't the one to make you settle,
but you cast me aside
excited for the feeling of someone else.

There's a part of me that questions
where my self-respect has gone,
How foolish I must have been to assume
This could never happen to me.

Your touch alone
Could save me from everything,
I wish I could indent the feeling of your fingertips
Into my skin,
Just to prove how vital it is to my anatomy.

For a long time, I had been stuck
In long stretched days
Rotting through blankets
And unchanged sheets,
But when you grabbed my hands
Into the palms of yours,
I swear I experienced a new dream
One I hadn't known I could want.

You scooped me out of the rubble
That had fallen on top of me
And held me till I regained the strengths of my limbs,
Letting me learn again what it was like to breathe through
Fresh air,
Helping me become a person again.

Can I be inside of your mind
For a little while
Just to see if it thinks like mine,
Would you be honest
Or is the truth not one of your specialties?

I wish I could see your real opinion of me,
The unfiltered one
That you never say out loud.

I study the way your body moves
To see if your feelings for me,
Go beyond the words you pick out
And I stare at your eyes
To see if they hold any disinterest.

We'd been on the same path
Side by side,
Without knowing each other
And when we collided,
Nothing felt normal again
Everything I thought I knew,
Became something I had to re-learn.

You made me look twice at things
Because somehow,
I missed you through the cracks
And now I'm worried I'll miss something again,
If I don't hold your hand.

We won't remember any of this in the morning
So, we cross every boundary
We have carefully stacked,
You're taking all you can get
And I'm too desperate
To even think about letting go.

It feels different
And all of a sudden,
we've ruined each other for anyone else,
We don't hear those thoughts in our heads
Telling us that maybe it's one-sided,
We just keep taking
Till we've memorised the feeling of it being like this.

I can tell in your eyes
That you want this as much as I do,
That you feel me in your bones
Like a sharp string of a violin.

Everything I do
Is a proclamation to you
When I tint my lips,
It's so you can't resist looking at them
And when I laugh,
I turn my head wondering if you saw.

You're always walking away
Thinking it's all one-sided on your end
When all I want is your hand,
Your smile,
Your late-night thoughts
And to be the reason you feel excitement.

Trust me I know you,
You may say that I don't
But I've read you inside out
Almost a hundred times.

I've memorised your lines
And the sounds you make,
Words that I play in my mind
As if it's my favourite song.

The only thing is
you never bothered to read me once,
So, while you may be my greatest fascination
I'm worried that you think of me as nothing but something
To make you feel good about yourself.

It's different arms
But they have no body heat,
It's the same position you once held me in
But I don't feel anything.

You have the same shade of eyes
But these ones mean nothing
And yours once meant everything.

I just want it to be you
But it's not
And it never will be,
As long as I keep replacing you with lookalikes
It will never be the real thing.

These words will never forget us,
They'll see us through
If we were to become extinct,
I've written down every smile you've given me
In case I ever don't know you.

You make me want to write a book as long as time,
Just to make people understand
Everything there is to love about you.

How there's always a light,
That comes from your company
And a home to go to,
When you are near.

I don't think anything will ever feel as right
As the way your arms do,
A song will never compare
To the way your laugh booms,
You've become the only thing I dream about
And a wish that only appears when the stars
Form rare constellations.

I've always been afraid of the way I would fill
The rest of my days,

But you make it easier
You make it exciting
Because to think that there might be a life
Where you want to call me yours,
Forever,
Well, I hope I get the privilege of experiencing it.

We had now become a past-tense
That had happened centuries ago,
Where I wrote movies
And you told me your stories.

I no longer get to experience any future memories of you
But I have all the old ones stocked up in a video player,
In the back of my mind
Ready to press play at any time.

We choose to ignore the impact we had on each other's lives,
But it's with me everyday
In the way I see life,
There is not a single thing you have said to me
That could go forgotten,
Or a touch that my body has lost the feeling of.

Nobody could love me
The way you once did
And not a soul could see mine,
For all it was.

Only yours knows it all,
Only yours could hold me till all my parts
Got glued back together
As if they never fell apart.

I always think about what my life could've been like
Had I not remained afraid,
Had I have jumped at the chance to be with you,
Told people how I felt
And not filtered versions of what I thought they wanted to hear.

I presume my life would have been a lot louder
With you in it,
Music would always be playing
And the happy kind
That makes you smile till your cheeks hurt.

I hope you are out there giving that kind of love
To someone else
Because you always had so much of it to give.

Sometimes on lonely nights
I like to indulge in a fantasy,
Making up memories for us
That goes beyond our cut-off date
And sometimes I torture myself with hope,
That maybe you will come back for me
Force me to do something outside of my comfort zone,
Like spending forever wasting time with you.

There are so many parts of me
Stolen in nights
And gained through memories,
There is a special piece of me I keep from others
Filled with your special touch
And though we are no longer,
I keep it inside of me
At all times,
Igniting it when all I want is to remember
Your presence.

I never knew I could feel such comfort from a person
Till you accidentally stumbled right into my life,
With your adorable mannerisms
And desperate need for conversation.

I could sit and do nothing
Till my heart gave out,
If your voice was filling my ears
And my space occupied you.

Every regret and accomplishment I have made,
Coincidentally tied a string connecting us together
And it's made all the breakdowns,
Unfulfilled dreams and tears
Worth having,
If it brought you to me.

All I want to do now
Is enjoy the simple things,
Like feeling the breeze kiss the strands of my hair
Because now I can relax,
You have made my world a fairy-tale
That I don't ever want to escape.

I'm afraid that you'll never like me as much as you did
On the night we first met,
That your interest in me will run out
Like sand flowing through an hourglass.

Maybe you will never find me as interesting
As you did that night,
With how quick you were to delve into a conversation
And continue it long into the next day.

I'm worried that I easily bore people
And that you might just be like the rest,
I don't know what to do
To make you like me forever
Because liking someone is different than loving someone,
But I want to try
Because all I want to do is make conversation with you,
Till our voices come out lost and forgotten.

I'm trying to hold onto what little hope I do have left
Pretending I don't care
And telling people when it finds me it finds me,
But they don't know I look for it in the most mundane of things.

I look for you
Hoping you exist
And that you hurry up and come and meet me already,
So, I can love someone like I've always wanted to.

It was such a build-up of anticipation
Between lips and another pair of lips,
It was years overdue
Until it wasn't
And it was happening in the present tense.

It was just two muscles
And it didn't matter that they belonged to you and me,
Neither did all the stuff that happened in between.

It was simple
And it made sense,
In a way nothing ever had before.

I hadn't been in the right place for so long
Especially when you knew me,
I was trapped in the cage I had abandoned myself in,
Till one day I made a key and I flew as far away as I could
From whom I used to be.

I wonder if you saw me now
You would be proud of the ways I changed,
There aren't a lot of times I think about you
But when I catch myself smiling about our shared memories,
I start hoping that one day
There will be a clear path leading us back,
Into each other's lives.

When we first met
I desperately begged and yearned
To something bigger than myself,
For you to start a conversation with me
That was all I wanted,
I hadn't dared to wish for anything else.

When you finally spoke a sequence of words
Directed at me,
I nearly collapsed inside
Trying to keep myself together,
Endlessly grateful that I was under your attention.

Nothing would come of it in the morning,
But it plagued my mind every once and a while
When I wanted to feel something.

We'll never say anything real
Is what I've come to terms with,
You'll act as if everything is so insignificant
And I'll never tell you how I feel
But we will coat ourselves in all this dishonesty,
Till our last breaths.

We are just always pretending, pretending
And pretending
To the point where neither of us
Knows whose line comes next.

You'll cover me whole
And even in this state of vulnerability
I still have no idea who you really are,
I'll sit with the facts
And you will dust yourself off,
Read to fade away
Contributing to our loss.

You put me in a corner
Where I am never fine with myself,
Casually tracing your footprints
To see if mine still looks like yours,
Hunting you down in places
That I know you're not around.

Playing songs, you used to listen to
Because they still mean something to me
And I'm losing hair,
When you're not even losing sleep.

There was no cure
I learnt over time,
Trying to get over you
Was something I couldn't rush
It had to happen slowly in little reminders
And awkward encounters.

As much as I wanted to stop thinking about your face
It allowed me to relish in my own raw pain,
I hope one day your name doesn't make me wince
But rather spreads a smile over my face
For what has been.

I know we supposedly hate each other
In the minute we are upon,
But I'm a liar
And I can lie enough for the both of us.

I'm telling people it happened for a reason
When I don't care about the lesson,
I'd rather live in ignorance
If it meant I could keep you.

I wanted to dig at my skin
And rip it clean of every part
That craved you,
In all my honesty
I didn't know how to be a person anymore
Because my whole existence,
Became consumed by you.

I was no longer a person,
I was a shell of want
And nothing else,
But you were still a person
And in place of my agony,
You felt nothing.

I was wasting away
Losing every inch of me to ridiculous feelings,
Foolishly pining over you till all of my parts had grazes
And you were just walking around,
oblivious to the torture
You put me through.

We are both too traumatised
To say the right thing,
We'll always have the wrong timing
And ignore each other,
Until we feel an overwhelming urge of want
And sadness,
From the time we aren't filling together.

We repeat the same lines
Every act,
Saying it doesn't matter
That we can move on,
Even though we know that as long as one of us
Is near,
We will cement our feet into the ground
Just in hope, we can still catch glimpses
Of each other.

I didn't want to have self-preservation
With you
Because I just wanted you to know me
And I'm not sure if you cared that much,
About finding out every crack of me
But I wanted to study your parts,
Till I memorised each fragment.

I didn't regret telling you everything
And never keeping a secret to myself,
Even if I tried
I no longer knew how to not tell you all of my
Thoughts
And I only hoped that you gladly longed for them.

I wanted to tell you something earnest,
Something that didn't seem
Like a bunch of words copied from someone else,
I wanted to make up my own language
Just to say how I felt in a way,
No one had told someone
Before.

You were worthy of that
Of a whole new language,
Filled with unique adjectives
That didn't belong to anyone except you.

I felt like I knew every secret
The world had to hold,
When you went away and came back
And looked at me
As if I was some life-changing event,
Like something you couldn't believe was real.

We didn't know how to speak
Or who touches who first,
Do we hug or do we turn around and walk
Our separate ways?

I learnt more about anything
I had come to known
In those five seconds,
Five seconds of realising every speck of existence
Until every second evaporated,
Falling so eloquently
And in their place,
Came your footsteps patiently making their mark
Towards me.

I'd run away with you
Till minutes forgot to pass
And our bones lost all their density,
I'd blindly forget everything
That I've ever been taught,
Just to feel you once more.

I'd collapse and die over and over again
So that I could hear you calling my name,
I just don't want to be anybody
If it means being someone you don't know.

I'm desperate
And hanging on by all of my agony
Just hoping that we get this right,
That something falls into place
So that we can have this night.

I was normal
Until one day you changed the way I existed,
You gave me things I hadn't begged to want
Or even been given the chance to hope for
And it was everything,
Every word out there.

It was all made up of things I couldn't explain
But it was simple
And I think for the time it lasted,
It could have been love
Or something short of it.

Now I don't complain that it went away
Or how it couldn't have lasted long enough,
I've accepted you as a memory
And even though I'm constantly making new ones
So far and different from it,
You'll always be my favourite.

There were so many beautiful things that I had seen
And I looked till I had my fill
Never considering that I was part of that category,
But you put me in it
Refusing to argue.

I wonder now if our time apart
Has forced you to put me in another category,
I hope not
But if you're bitter
Then I'll be ugly for you,
Just on the off chance that it makes you happy.

And I wonder if when we fall accustomed
To the tragedy of time
If you'll surprise me,
By ruining every memory
For the spell of something young.

I know through history repeats
And tales as old as time,
That I'll ripen
With more curved lines and skin
That fails to show any resistance.

So, I wonder if you'll behave
Or you'll treat our decay as an act of insanity
And leave me for something,
That reminds you of a life
With too many years ahead of it.

We only had one season,
One season of memorising all of each other's
Expressions
Telling secrets till we forgot that the night
Wanted us to sleep,
But each day meant exploring more of what
Was not known the day before.

I'll have you during this sun
But I won't have you by the time the leaves fall,
We both knew that
And as we're miles away from that deadline
We didn't care about getting too close,
Until one of us gets burnt.

We laughed while we kissed
And always got distracted
With more questions,
While the summer left us with golden skin
And fresh valleys of freckles,
It also left us immortal for the time being.

Soon enough
We will find all of this too cliché
And the mysteries we discovered in each other

Will someday bore us,
Till we move on to our clothed layers and hiding ourselves
And then one day summer will come again,
Reminding us to miss the heat that we encountered.

There was so much time we filled without
Each other,
That we waited to find out the details we missed
What truths had shaped us,
When our communications had fizzled out.

I craved them predictably
Every time,
Hoping that something would remind you of me
Just so that I could tell you,
How I was a completely different person.

I felt like we had gone through so many
Different versions of one another,
That it was as if we were always
Reverted back to strangers.

We always sprung into a different form
With every passing year
And when we no longer talked,
I often found myself wondering about what the length of your hair was
Or what clothes you were now wearing?

I miss you
And maybe that's an obvious thing
But it's no longer just words anymore,
I feel my longing in torturous amounts
as if it's taking over my whole body,
That there is no more room for me to have any other thoughts.

All I do is carry that with me,
Through every room I enter
And on every travel, I make,
Being as desperate as ever
For you to appear in every circumstance,
Even though I know you won't
But I count down the seconds anyway
And beg to be surprised.

I might not seem like the same girl anymore
Or whomever I was when you met me,
But I tried to be
I thought it would be nice to forget for a moment,
That time had me morphing into something entirely new.

Even though everything is so different
And it's become hard to smile at things
That you don't recognise,
You've come to peace with knowing that if I
Walk out that door,
You won't realise it when I come back.

One day you'll learn to keep your doors locked
And forever you will live with not knowing
Who I am,
Or what I seem to be doing
And whether that leaves you in anguish or peace,
I'll never know.

We were too late to realise
That we wanted each other,
That by the time any of our feelings made sense
We had fallen into different arms.

When the morning had seen us through,
Swept us from the rug we were standing on
Into a morning we felt brand new to,
We knew that now everything would be so
Very different to what it has been.

Losing all sense of familiarity
We were stumbling through crowded streets
And watching people we wished we could be,
Maybe you were bitter
Or you felt little to no indifference,
It's possible that I was all alone
in my newfound sense,
That I wasn't equipped to handle.

I felt crucified by the night
That I learned to be terrified of it,
Worried that every time I wasn't secured
In the sunlight,
You'd be there at my door
Waiting to take something you didn't care much for
Away.

When the past just becomes a story,
Will you trace your palms and think of me
Do you touch your lips,
And feel the permanent stain of me?

I'll always be everywhere you are,
The parts of me you wanted to keep
Scattered in every secret hiding space,
You can think of
So, you don't have to explain why,
So, that you can keep me for yourself
Even after years passed,
That you begged to slow down.

You'll put on a brave front,
An act to anyone you are ever destined to meet
And you lie to whomever you kiss,
That it means as much as it once had
But you know in the cuts,
That has weakened your heart
That if it's not me,
You will always feel
The triumph of defeat.

Silent conversations
And swollen lips,
Tired cheekbones
And the music that sounds like it was
Written for us.

Suns that feel like jackets when you're cold
And nights that remind you of your youth,
Kisses that end with you feeling deprived,
Hugs that mean something
And dancing to a song you feel in your bones.

My name being called by you
And my mouth calling the syllables of your name
Right back.

Between us are the words
We don't want to say,
But there's no more comfort in our silences anyway
And we're too caught up in everything
That keeps us apart
Because the longer we aren't together,
It feels better these days.

I went from falling into you
To breaking down
And now I can't wait any longer,
Because I'm so utterly
Tired of turning into different shapes
Just by any movement you make.

When we consume ourselves into the hour we are upon,
Do we hesitate to acknowledge
That is all we have been doing,
Is forcing patterns to appear
So that we can point out a sign,
That so evidently reveals that this is right.

Maybe there is no pattern to this
It could be something that is so random,
That there is no sequence for it
And that's the scariest part
That neither of us has a script,
For whatever is to come next.

But there is something to be said
About how much hope we have for something
So entirely trivial,
That we throw ourselves into every meaning
And every chance
Just to come out of it all,
Holding hands.

Maybe if we lay on our backs long enough
We can outthink ourselves
And detonate the hardwire,
That makes us think till we can't rest.

Maybe we could mean something to each other,
Just enough to have one pathetic reason
For us to be able to get through a day,
You'll taste the desperation on my tongue
And I'll make up that it's something I've had to drink.

I almost said hello to you today
My hand almost rose,
Till I willed it to forget its muscles.

My eyes begged to search you,
So, I forced them to forget they ever
Knew you.

Don't Leave Me Here

We were torn before you sliced the knife
You died slowly by my side
Until nothing was left of us,
Only a title obliging our bodies, to be stuck in such despair.

I missed you in pictures even when you were near,
Goosebumps were permanently placed on my body
In the ghost of where your hands used to touch,
Too soon were we stuck into dull maturity
That we forgot what it was like to feel any sort of excitement.

Even still as we stand in rotting bones,
My patience is outdrawn in hopes that we can go back
And reclaim our past.

When the glass shatters all over the floor
You try to pick it up,
But it slices your fingers in the act
So, you try to fix it,
To not feel the damage, it has inflicted.

Except it always leaves a scar
And the skin is never the same,
It has thicker skin and darker edges
So, you cry because you feel how much you miss
Your old skin,
As if the wound has managed to thread itself into
Every vantage points.

Now there is no longer glass on the floor,
But you feel the memories on your fingertips
And although it never feels normal again,
You learn to kiss the scar
Without delving into everything that has been
That will never come again.

It was seen by everyone
The way we interacted,
People would say it was
so clear how in love you were with me
But no one knew the things they couldn't see.

They didn't see the shades you had splattered me with
Or the words you said
To break me into dust,
I was strong but not enough compared to you
So, no one could see
That what we had
Was not some kind of puppy love.

It's crazy how slowly time goes by
But how quickly months fly past,
How you can call something infinite
Like you and me
Even though there was always going to be,
an invisible expiry date.

I've forgotten the feeling of being with you
But nevertheless
The pictures are still in frames,
How different we must have been back then
To have enjoyed each other's company,
When now we use the house,
we bought
To hide from each other.

On the first night we met,
Your hands touched me
As if they had never touched anything else,
Pads of fingers met curves of mine
We couldn't get enough
Collapsing each night into what we thought
could be the end.

Time started to pass
While my skin became familiar,
Something you decided to hate the feeling of
And every room I entered
Became one you exited.

When you first encountered me
I was new
Something different,
A shiny toy
Somebody worth talking to and having around.

Except I became old
As soon as you had worn me out,
Now everyone else is new
And I'm just an extra weight you carry.

One you want to toss when your eyes lay upon
Someone else,
That has a shade of eyes you aren't used to.

And though my mind is aware of this
I wait and stay
Hoping you change,
That you look at me again
And appreciate what you have,
But each day that comes
Disappointment is all I find and the realisation,
That I'll never be new to you again.

You've turned me into a fool
Making me tell anyone who could hear
That you were different,
Making me believe that you really wanted me
For more than a month's span.

But as soon as March came
So did I in your eyes,
You tossed me out for some other prize
And now I feel ashamed of the days I thought you felt lucky
To have me,
When all I have now is the same old repeated history.

Why don't you kiss me,
Like it's all you want?

Why is a small gesture never enough?

It's only ever forceful hands
Grabbing anywhere they can,
Till you're all over me
And there isn't a bit of me left.

I wish one day
You would touch me gently
Graze my skin like I'm an antique piece,
But you only ever throw me around
And remind me that I should be grateful
Someone wants to touch me.

Every time someone new comes along
I can't help but hope that it will be something different,
But as moments begin to shift
And start overlapping
You make me a fool,
For ever thinking you were something beyond
Anything I had ever experienced.

It's all over now
Everything we ever knew,
A year passed and we turned into adults
Something we knew nothing about,
We forgot our old friendships
The songs that made us cry
And the crushes we never talked to.

Our brains matured and detached themselves from any enthusiasm
So, all we could do was think about the past
And somewhere along the lines of reminiscing,
We forgot every hardship we'd been through
Because it had been covered up by nostalgia.

It all became just a foggy memory of being young
And having indescribable dreams,
That never seemed like they were out of reach.

You were the only thing I trusted
Even though you weren't human,
It didn't matter
You were just made up of soft surfaces
And kind loving eyes.

In simple forms, you were the most beautiful thing to me,
Every day you kept the same sparkle in your eye
Your fascination for the world never died,
You were my best friend
And we only ever needed each other's company.

But loving you could only ever be temporary,
Because you had a short timeline
And I tried to clasp the years in my hand,
To stop whatever force of ageing
from dragging you down.

Eventually, time couldn't wait
and you slipped out of my hands,
Even though I never got to say goodbye.

Even in a week's time
I can forget how you felt under the palms of my hands,
They mourn the feeling of you
And try to touch something that appears as the same texture.

Except it's never enough
It all feels slightly altered
And each day that passes away,
The more I forget the feeling
But if I could tattoo it into my bones,
I would
Because forgetting is something too heartbreaking to do.

A house feels empty without you
It's no longer a home when I can't hear you,
Walls are breathing loudly
But no sound compares to yours.

I'm alone with the dust now,
It creeps into my hair
And I walk through abandoned corridors
That no longer end with you.

You never really can say goodbye
One last moment
Is never enough,
It only lasts a couple of fleeting seconds
And is gone before it starts.

But being with you is a feeling I can't forget
The only problem is it will never come again,
As long as I have my memory intact
You'll be forever stitched in my body and mind
And I'll make a timeline,
That sees us all the way through
Next time.

It's funny how different we mean to each other,
I was just a part of one of your routines
But you were the only thing getting me through the week.

I'm not sure if I ever excited you
But you never failed to thrill me,
So, I cherish the days you feature in
And let myself be an insignificant speck,
In your ever-changing life.

Her skin is flaked
But she shines with jewellery,
There are bones protruding
And wine-stained tongues.

A husband is out drinking
With girls that have barely left their adolescence,
They buy
And they weep
Living outside of a daydream,
Their eyes do not lock
And their tempers are boiling hot.

A house with too many rooms,
Locked up secrets,
Deposits,
Lonely halls looming to different destinations
It's a horrific play of perfection.

It's hard to stick around
When all you've ever done is tear me apart,
But I can't leave you
Because leaving you is like,
ditching a nostalgic part of me
And departing means I've grown too much.

You would hate it if someone betrayed you
Like you've always done to me,
I must have turned into some kind of masochist
To have let someone in so much,
Just for them to eventually run out.

It's so easy for you to go on without me
But for me, it hurts more as days keep
Spreading themselves out,
How is it that we could face such different impacts from each other,
But that I would be the one dealing with our past.

If we ever found each other again
And things were aligned
No obstacles clouding your way,
I wonder if that would have made you stay.

Some part of me thinks I'm missing a core part of human emotions
One of the purest forms,
That I am not capable of falling in love
So, I'm just pretending to feel things,
To make up for what I'm lacking.

What is the point of missing out on heartbreak
And midnight confessions,
If it saves our feelings
But reminds us that we are human?

If I can't stimulate these things
Does that make me a robot?

Did I hack the initial coding,
Or have I just starved myself
Of any potential happenings?

Can you imagine if we never met
If each night you made me cry
Was replaced with nights,
I had spent living my life.

Or was I always destined to be introduced to someone
Like you?

A life ruiner,
Turning everyone into a human treadmill
For your worn-out feet.

I'm sure there's a line of people that share your words
And ill-timed jokes,
But what if I met the one behind you
Would it still have been a mistake?

I want to hear you say the words
That will make up for all of this space
We have between us,
But every time I ask
I get angry
Because you say so much,
Without saying anything worthy.

Maybe I'll just have to accept
That we've reached the end,
Even though I never had time to prepare
So, was it all a waste?

Every memory we made up
Tell me,
what made you
Betray me in such a way?

It's horrible having to know
Two versions of you,
When I grief one of them
Even when the other is standing in front of me,
You've changed so much
That I don't see myself fitting your lifestyle
Anymore.

Your past clones
Would have never stood for everything
You've become
But you destroy their voices,
In waves of alcohol
And the promise of people liking you.

I guess I can't blame you
When you have finally achieved
Being seen by others,
I just wish that didn't mean
Turning your back on me.

I always wondered how people's lives got better
After they had just hurt someone,
It seemed cruel to watch them exist
And see their fortunes overload
While their victims were stuck,
With pained expressions and deep misery.

Although you and I may never speak again
We are strung together through memories,
Through past versions of ourselves
That no one else will ever get to meet,
I loved you completely with every version I had become
But stopped short when we came across eighteen.

There will never be a moment
That I can take back,
Because every talk of running away
And moving to different countries,
Led me to everything that is my present
Every regret and outcome,
Whether it was really for the better.

A two-syllable word
Never properly fixed anything
And we obviously weren't an exception,
It's utterly devastating
That we have to learn how to avoid each other,
Something I wish you never made me do.

I think about you when I'm sleeping
Even more when you don't want to talk to me,
I hate that you've made me a hobby
When I've put you over everything.

There are plenty like me
Who pine and lose sleep over you
And I'm a part of the list,
Of those waiting
For you to want them.

Meeting me,
means nothing to you
But for me it's rare
I'm trying to get over it but each time I try,
My hope steps in
Thinking that maybe,
I'm someone you'll miss.

I'm burying so many feelings
Ones that cross from anger and disbelief,
I want them gone
They have to be in order for us to exist.

It doesn't seem to be working
And forgiveness doesn't set me free,
Even when you hold me close
I feel them overcoming my restraints.

You have nothing to accept
Or to get over
But you have given me those obstacles.

What am I supposed to do with all this hurt
That has forced itself,
Into the space we leave
Between us.

Did you do it on purpose?
To make me hate you
Or was it a careless act,
One you could make again if the timing fit
You apologise for hurting me,
But you don't know how to make it better.

What am I supposed to do with
All these unsolved answers?
When you don't have so much as a motive
Or band-aids in hand.

You haven't even realised,
That your hands have turned into knives
And although we stopped sitting in silence,
You never stopped stabbing old scars.

I'm trying to like you,
My head is telling me
That is what should happen,
When someone likes you
You like them back.

But my heart can't stand it,
I don't want to be with you
But if I don't want to,
Does that mean that there is
Something wrong with me?

Are my parts wired incorrectly?
And now I can't be with anyone
Who wants to be with me?

I was waiting till everything worked out
There was nothing I could do to stop fleeing,
From all my unmade decisions
There were people I had let go
And they had moved on with their lives.

If I could do it all again,
I'm not sure I would make a choice
That would be worth making.

But if I could stop time
I'd spend it holding a conversation with you,
Just to hear the way syllables roll out of your mouth.

I'm pretending strangers are my friends
Giving them too much information
Because there is no one else to tell,
They listen and for a brief moment
It means something to them.

I never let strangers in too much,
Just enough so that they keep listening
And so I can open my mouth
For the day.

I try so hard
Just to get you to like me,
I smile and walk behind you
So, you don't get mad,
I'm walking on eggshells constantly
Hiding from myself.

You always complain about me
So, I make sure to be extra nice
To make my company better for you,
I just wish I didn't have to do anything
And you could for once, stay calm
Or appreciate that I'm still here.

You always get the best
And leave me with whatever is left,
Dissociating is my way out of everything
Because I don't want to remember this feeling.

Why do I keep punishing myself,
For your unstableness?

There is something so different
About making friends when you get older,
Becoming close with people who didn't
Witness your coloured braces,
That haircut you had that made you insecure,
Your first crush
And how strict your parents were.

Even though they've become the first ones you'd call,
There is a certain nostalgia
About old friends,
That they will never be able to restore.

I've put on shiny clothing
Painted my face with your favourite colours,
But yet still
that doesn't turn your eyes towards me,
I try so hard to be directly in your line of vision
When I've never been on your radar.

I'm embarrassing myself
Every single time,
Counting my luck
And manifesting that one day,
I could become someone you fancy.

You seem to be friends with everyone
And I wait patiently for you to strike up a conversation
With me,
But it seems like when you do look at me
It's only done by accident,
Or when I'm in the way of someone you actually want.

There are no adolescent years of my life left,
I've spent them all up
And I waste my time now
Wishing I still had an inch of it back,
But now I've been replaced
The teenage girl I was,
Has now cast another lead.

I'm filled with envy
For those who still have those years left,
How they probably look for romance in every room
And don't have a mind
trying to find every reason why there is something
so clearly wrong.

You turned me into a villain
With your untruthful devotions,
You acted as if loving me was a foolish thing
For you to do
But then begged at my feet,
Whenever I left.

I can't seem to look at the reflections
Without a glimpse of your face
Trespassing my mind,
You begged me to like you
And then left like you never said anything.

Now I'm in a car
With some stranger pretending it's you,
Just to get through the night
But their touches never seem to feel
Like yours.

My greatest act
Was pretending to be everything I'm not,
All at once
Making you think I was funny,
By trying to say too many useless things
At the same time
Until you laughed,
Desperate for a good reaction.

I've realised now I've lost myself in the act
And I'm not sure what parts
Are actually me.

I just don't want to be your entertainer anymore
All I want is to be quiet
And for it to still be enough
for you to irrevocably need me.

You want it all
Without giving much,
You like everything to rely on the physical
But I just want to hear the way you think about things.

You only like me when something is revealed
So, I offer it,
Until I'm not sure when my boundaries have been crossed
And you're saying I did a good job.

Sometimes I think about your company in the mornings,
What you would be like when the sun is out
But you never grant me that,
You only know me when the moon has arrived.

My tears had run dry
I sat on a darkened bench
Waiting to wake up,
Waiting till I stopped tingling
And for someone who knew me
To arrive.

Then you came
With the height that you had on me
And your beady eyes,
You never even asked me a question
You just grabbed my safety in the palm of your hands
And smashed it with the clench of your fingers.

I wish I had hid from you
Before your mouth decided to take mine,
But you craved someone innocent
Who had no inhibitions,
Someone who couldn't fight back.

I've accepted a lot of treatment
I know others wouldn't tolerate,
All because I crave when nice things
Come out of your mouth.

I wait like a dog
Hoping you throw me something,
Sitting at your feet when you don't
And giving you space when you hate me.

Everyone tells me I've lost it,
Letting you trick me into obedience
But they don't know how stuck I am
Because I don't want to leave you early,
Just in case you decide to change.

How foolish have I become
Waiting for a day that will probably never come,
When all my friends have their loved ones
Holding them near
And kissing their pains away,
Instead of inflicting them.

Show me that you are still here,
Throw something at me
Do anything,
At least show me you're still breathing
It's too awfully silent,
Now that my days don't end with you.

Hurt me
Just to prove that you still exist,
That you are still the person I knew you to be
That we haven't grown into complete strangers,
With all these wasted memories.

Haunt me
So that I know you still think of me,
That you still want a bar of me
That I'm not someone you regret,
Just don't leave me alone forever
Because I can't bear to be ignored by you.

You didn't see it as I did
Everyone told you how bad you had to crave it
But I was told to always save it.

To me, it was the most vulnerable thing a person could ever go through
Not being able to hide behind materials,
Or misdemeanours
But you saw it as nothing special
And you tricked me into thinking I could change your perspective,
Except I saw the look in your eyes
Mine were tearing up
And yours were dry.

I just became a story
One that only you would tell,
I became dirty
A person ripped outside of a shell.

Everything always feels off
The lights are always too bright
And if they aren't they're too dim,
Moments are always too short
That you stay for seconds too long,
Till you shouldn't be in it anymore.

You don't know when the appropriate time is
To leave something behind
Or if you're leaving something too early,
It's horrible having to deal with all this indecision
All this mess.

Everything that you've scraped under the rug
And things that you wish would come back again,
Feelings you want to drown yourself in
Ages you want to relive.

Pretending to be content
and that you're okay with where you are,
Telling yourself that you're fine with situations
When all you want to do is run away all the time.

Convincing yourself you like people
When you just feel like a robot telling people what you think

They want you to say,
Having to heal from things
And waiting for a faster approach to find you.

Someone to tell you what to do
Someone to blame for your stupidity,
A flame to throw your fears in
A blanket to hide you
So that you don't have to be anything,
So that you can just be a person living
Without any choices to make
Or any expectations to live up to,
Or to be able to sleep at night
And not wake up tired.

I've become a puppet on a string
Just for your affections,
You tell me you like something
And I'll try my hardest to be it,
I change everything
My hair
Clothes
And my jokes,
So that I can morph into something you want.

It never works
But I'm still on your string
Altering myself,
In case one day it does
One day when I'm not invisible
Or you see me before you see others,
But until then I'm just an awful chameleon
Changing colours to suit you,
When you don't even notice.

It's funny how a certain song can always
Take me back,
How I can forget everything I once felt
Every person I used to dream about,
But as soon as one intro fades in
I'll remember it as if it never left me.

Like for one second, I'm back
And I'm that old version of myself
Till the seconds turn into milli ones
And there's no sound,
Then I'll forget once again.

I'm always hidden
Whether it's in a corner,
Secluded in my bedroom of my own sentenced quarantine
Or the shadow of the person next to me.

I stay silent,
Too cautious of what move must be made next
Worried that if I make too much sound,
I'll be a disruption
So, I don't speak and I don't ask for anything
And I keep to myself,
Thinking that even making eye contact with anyone
Could possibly burn them.

I'm always watching others have their moments
Already accepting that my moments will only be secrets,
I've lost count of the times I've been a spotlight
Ensuring that you pay attention to anything
That isn't me,
But for once I wish someone would turn off that light
And see what hides behind it.

I wake up and I have my meal planned
And I go through the day with a numbness written all over my face,
Walking too fast even though I have nowhere to be
Blinking back the hours I didn't sleep
And driving through endless streets.

Nothing makes me feel alive anymore
Like how I used to feel
And I haven't been bothered to search for something
That sparks every vein in my body.

I've replaced the things that once felt like chasing
Down the world as if it would reveal us
it's secrets,
With more pointless to-do lists.

I spent all night
Flipping through questions in my head
Not letting a single thought be left unanswered,
I took everything as a sign
Or a symbol
Just to feel like I wasn't constantly stuck in my own ruining.

I tried to forget you
By leaving you on the last page of the book I read,
Trapping you in it
But you always found your way out
And as much as I tried to ignore how much
I thought about you,
There you were tempting me to put you back in.

I saw every pattern
Every trace of you sketched in every street
and even though I hoped I'd never run into you again,
there was always a thrill in the air
that begged for your presence.

From the first night I met you,
I didn't feel like I had my fill
I wanted more but I didn't know how to ask,
There was something holding me back
Beneath all my want
And desperation
But you were just always there,
Looking like not a thing could faze you.

I wanted to disguise my want
But as much as I tried it always came
Seeping through,
Making me grovel in despair
And punching my stomach to tell it to give me
Some rest.

Maybe I only became addicted to you
Because you never gave an inch back
And as much as I blame it on anything,
Besides myself
I hated that you weren't in just as much agony as me
And that whatever I had for you,
Wasn't contagious.

I'm not sure how many more words I can take,
I'll sit in silence while you throw every
Syllable you know at me
And I'll think that this time I'm done,
This time I will walk away
And leave you to give your words
To someone else.

Except another day comes
And I've forgotten every argument
Every commitment to myself,
Just to remember them by the end of the day.

You nit-pick everything about me
Till I'm not even sure you really know who I am,
I'm this
I'm that,
But I'll never be anything you like
I'm always just going to be your punchline.

I take it all with a straight face
Not inching a muscle
Even when you get mad at that,
I'm trying to say the right thing
But you always shut me up.

Just when I think I'm on the brink
Of cutting our threads
And locking you up,
You turn sweet for a moment
Muttering things, you probably don't mean
Putting on a show that I'll believe,
Tricking me into becoming yours again.

I wish I didn't have to beg for you to be nice
To me
But I do it pathetically anyway,
I give you everything
And I do whatever you say
As fast as you want me to,
Pushing over boundaries and every offence
Just to please you,
So, you'll pat me on the head.

I don't know how this started
How somewhere between the lines of false politeness
Came blunt aggression,
But I wish I'd never met you
Because then I'd never be trapped in the first place.

We used to be friends at first
And now I'm just your pushover,
Ready for you to abuse when you need to
Or ignore when you want to.

He lacked so many things
And he tried to fill those gaps,
By ripping them out of me
Because he thought that I was a dumping ground,
For the things he didn't want
And that he deserved my every piece.

There is so much want
I have
And it is leaking through me
As if someone forgot to close my lid,
My ribs hurt
And I'm so obsessive that I don't know how to feel okay
With anything.

I'm nothing to you
Not a single thing
But my angst has turned into a giant monster,
That wants to eat you alive
So, I'm keeping my distance
Because I can't bear to know,
That none of this means anything to you at all.

I stopped hoping for things
And I noticed
That I didn't care how my days came,
Or how I filled them
An hour became two
Till I had spent the whole night staying awake.

I stopped laughing
And it wasn't like I was sad
There was just nothing to feel anymore,
Every emotion and expression
Had been used to its exhaustion
And now there was no filter I could put on it,
I had run out of everything.

The past still feels like something I can grab a hold of
And throw myself into,
So, I'm not trying to make anything count right now
But I keep moving forward and forgetting
Memories one at a time,
Praying that maturing doesn't mean
Losing all of them.

After too many drunken conversations with you
I realised that I'll never be
The person you settle down with,
I'll always be reserved for the side of you
That drinks and smokes and rarely stays sober
But I'll never witness you as you are.

You only want me as your party girl
But you'd never do anything mundane with me,
I'm your escape
But I won't be here for long
Which was something you understood all along.

It didn't matter that I showed up
Or that I bought new things to wear
To make you see me through another lens,
You have made up your mind
That I'm easily forgettable
For when you want to up and leave.

I had never walked this path before,
There were many places
And feelings I experienced
But none of them were acquainted with this.

This was new and the most terrified I have ever been
Like I'd been spit out of the only thing I'd ever known
And been told to make something out of it,
But the thing is I don't know what that
Something is.

So now I'm just slowly orbiting,
Collecting up my fears
And regrets into one big cardboard box,
Ready to take to another destination.

I'm losing people I've known on the way
Dropping them off to never see them again
And I'm stuck with memories of them,
Till one day I forget the slopes of their faces.

Every time I was close to remembering
Something that had previously been
I wanted to grab it in my hands,
Force it into my vision
And throw myself there,
Before I distanced myself with too many years
And birthday candles.

I'm always hoping to feel how I have before
Trying so desperately to not act as if my age
Has progressed me from enjoying things,
But I'm always in the corner of reminiscing
Collecting sounds and smells,
That are slipping through my senses.

You don't remember it in all of its parts,
It comes back through
Memories of running through sunset streets,
Thinking that you'll be young forever.

Our memories are so hazy,
We don't recall the nights we cried
Or wanted so badly for it to be over,
We only pick out all the parts that made us infinite
Like how hanging out well into the night,
Made us feel like we were conquering every
Something,
That felt bigger than ourselves
And every song we liked,
Turned into a piece of our souls.

Now it's a painful pang in the chest
Because it all was so long ago
And nothing could quite replace it,
Every friendship was supposedly forever
That you forgot what it was like to be alone.

We don't know how to make memories anymore,
Or ones that count for anything
And now you don't know when the last time was,
That you had done something with
Company.

It never lasts forever
But you tried to stretch the time out,
Till your grip started to slip
And your muscles gave out,
But you tried to make it significant
And only months can prove that.

No matter how much you tried
To escape the ending
And remain in the beginning,
The end came
In all the nights you spent asleep,
So, you could wake
And find yourself thrown out
Before you could make sense of it.

If I cover myself in my childhood blankets,
Maybe I can escape the end for a little while
If I remain in familiar hallways,
Maybe I won't have to walk into one
I'm terrified of.

If I keep my old clothes,
Maybe it will keep me from growing older
If I sit on my couch woven through threads
That all have a story,
Maybe everything will learn to be okay.

I stopped living
And hit pause on being a person,
I gave myself a jail sentence
To sit and rot in all my self-sabotage
And I watched everyone else around
Making names for themselves,
As I stabbed my knife further to my chest.

I didn't care about the shortness of my breath
Or how I used to cry at any reflection,
I didn't have any reason
To exist anymore
And I couldn't try or act like I could be bothered,
To find one.

Maybe I always rushed into things
So that I could have a sense of belonging
For an hour,
But I never thought about the afters
That I was constantly submerged in,
Once everything eventually ended.

One day you'll remember it all
Without the subsequential pang,
That hits your chest
And maybe instead you'll be able to laugh,
Without all the existential dread.

The past is always happening
In the seconds where we've forgotten,
Of its existence
And somewhere along the line,
Every friendship you've loosely made
And kisses you've harboured,
Will forget its bounds and get lost on the way.